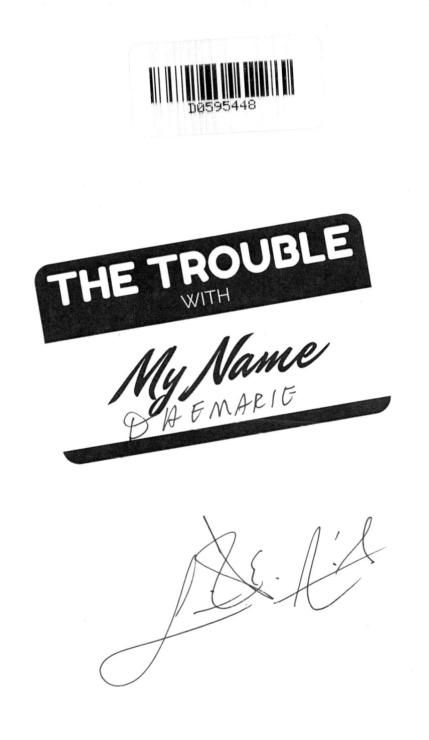

Javier Ávila

The Trouble with My Name

Poems from the One-man Show

Foredust Press

Published by Foredust Press. For *The Trouble with My Name* one-man show booking information or any questions regarding publishing content from this volume, contact info@javieravila.net.

www.javieravila.net

Cover Design by Michelle Cintrón

Cover Photo by Adam Atkinson

Some of the poems which appear in this volume first appeared in the following publications: *Vapor:* "Notes on the Death of My Father," "María de los Ángeles de la Cruz De Jesús," "Album," "Santurce," "Wake," "Certainties," "Weak Spot," "Bright Day," "Debt"; *Northampton Magazine:* "Denied Service"; *The Laconic:* "Grader Fear."

ISBN: 978-1-937149-30-7

Printed in the United States of America

for Oscar Paddock Ávila

Contents

*The benefits of speaking multiple languages
have been widely documented.
Nevertheless, some people take pride
in being linguistically ignorant.*

DENIED SERVICE

Upon being heard speaking Spanish
at the entrance of a restaurant in Hazleton, PA.

Should I have told the waitress
that my father never had a good night's sleep,
that he was haunted by recurrent nightmares
after that day when he, a young man
with stripes on his shoulders,
led Private Díaz and Private González
to the safety of the trenches,
and rescued Corporal Murphy, Private Williams,
and Private First Class De León
from the hovering claws of tanks and gunfire
before he tried and failed to save Private Rivera,
twenty-year-old Carlos Rivera, Carlitos,
beloved father of newborn María Rivera,
to whom he promised to return
safely from Korea? My father,
deafened by the shots, the shrieks of torture,
the agony of oscillating bullets,
dragged Carlitos' body through smoke and ashes,
saw the blood run in rivulets over the mud;

the tourniquet was not enough to stop the flow,
and as Carlitos bled to death, my father said:
Hold on, my friend. *Aguanta*
que pronto salimos de esto,
but they would not get out in time for life,
and for Carlitos, who whispered
mi María as his last breath,
that would be it. This cross
my father carried with him every day.

Should I have told the waitress
that my uncle lost both legs in Vietnam,
and that the phantom pain
no morphine could erase
—the throbbing of the stumps,
the constant pounding, sharp like a tornado,
relentless like the memory of war—
would follow him throughout the bitter journey
from opium to Prozac?
And a decade after his return to the island,
he still assured my mother
that the American Military Academy
was the best choice for me to learn
the discipline of service.

Should I have told the waitress
that both my father and my uncle,

who worked for the federal government,
died in the same Veterans Hospital
in Guaynabo, the same year
my cousin enlisted
in the US Marine Corps?

Should I have told the waitress
that after years with the JROTC
insignia on my sleeve
and a bilingual education on the island
that Spain forgot,
I now teach English to native English speakers
in North America,
the English that I learned in the Caribbean,
specifically the US Commonwealth
(yes, a commonwealth,
like the Commonwealth of Pennsylvania)
Puerto Rico
where I was born and raised?

Should I have told the waitress
that having this skin
that white people pay good money for
at the tanning salon
is not a crime?
That saying *salud* instead of "Bless you"
when someone sneezes

is not a crime?
That greeting friends with a kiss
instead of a handshake
is not a crime?
That teaching Spanish to my son,
who calls the mainland home,
is not a crime?
That I cannot remove the *plátano* stain on his back
nor would I want to
because he is the grandson of Sergeant Avila,
who sacrificed his health for us,
who didn't let Carlitos die in vain,
who taught me well the value
of silence
and of words,
who knew since he was the same age as this woman
who has already judged me
that there are things in this world
that cannot be denied.
Soy ciudadano de los Estados Unidos.
Y soy puertorriqueño.

Should I have told the waitress
anything
when she called me
a foreigner?

I was born and raised in Puerto Rico.
Until I moved to the mainland,
I was white.

PRIDE OF OWNERSHIP

Trimming the rose bush for the first time,
I wear rubber gloves, and use the shears
my father in law had recommended.

This summer morning in Bethlehem,
two cardinals perched upon the lowest branch
of the sycamore, observe
as I whistle the way any new homeowner
in 2006 would whistle,
with no recession in sight.

Across the street, my neighbor struts past his Audi,
with a full head of white hair,
and the skin of a chap who spends Saturdays
at the country club.
He nods his head and says,
"Nice work."

I smile, remove my gloves,
and say, "Hi. Nice to meet you.
I'm Javier."

"What a coincidence," he replies.
"My guy's name was José.
Great Mexican fella!
Had to go back, you know.
Your English is pretty good. Better than his.
Listen, I live right there,
in the one with the hydrangeas.
When you're done with this one,
could you come over and give me
an estimate?"

Student from Puerto Rico: "Professor, what's the meaning of maiden name?"

Student from Pennsylvania: "Professor, why didn't your wife take your last name?"

MARÍA DE LOS ÁNGELES DE LA CRUZ DE JESÚS

is
not
an atheist
by accident.

Apathy can be the most dangerous element in a college classroom.

THE DROP

If at the very moment that your waiter
is serving you the cup,
from his gleaming, drenched forehead,
an obese drop of sweat
descends into your coffee,
would you drink it?

Surely you would not.
I can see your aversion.
But I would.
Yes, I would drink the coffee
because inside the liquid
there is only a minuscule element
extraneous and repugnant.
The rest is only quality.

And all this, so that you understand, Anastasia,
that I cannot be hurt by your apathy.
You are merely the drop
of sweat
in my classroom.

If a tree falls in the forest,
and it doesn't take a selfie,
did it really fall?

FACEBOOK POEM

I am just like you, only better.
I have two-thousand seven hundred
more friends than you
and I baked an awesomely delicious,
deliciously awesome,
delsomely awlicious,
aliciously dawsome carrot cake tonight.
And it got six hundred likes in five hours.
And seven hundred of you know
I ran five miles this morning.
Five point three.

Let's keep it real. I'm happy.
Look.
I'm happy.
There is evidence of that.
You can see it by the smile
on my nine hundred and forty-five
profile pictures.
You can see that I am happier than you.
And my kids are happier than yours.
Take a look at the three dozen

family selfies (famfies)
we took at Vito's pizzeria.
Look. There's Vito in the background.
And there we are, looking good.
Check out the tan.
And the pizza was perfection.
Vito made it himself.
He said, "I make it especial
just for your family!"
And boy did he ever.
Every slice. Special indeed
from tip to crust.
Our pie tastes better than your pie.

When we go out with friends,
forget about it!
Because you know
we are having a better time than you.
Is anybody frowning?
You can see it here. Right here.
This album
of one hundred and twenty pictures
cannot lie.
#tooblessedtobedepressed
This is Joy.

Scroll down for more and more,

more ecstasy, more laughter. More.
And more.
We captured everything. More.
Nothing was wasted. More.
It all was documented for the future
because
we're making history right here.

Scroll down and see
how at the meat section
of the grocery store,
we party hard;
how in the dentist's waiting room,
we party hard;
and at the forty-five minute traffic jam on 22,
we party hard;
at little Riley's dance recital,
we party hard.
At newborn Madison's swimming lesson,
we party hard.
At Brady's soccer practice,
we party hard.
At the breast-cancer 5K
(that's us right there, eating hot dogs),
we party hard.
And next to Grandma
dying in a hospital bed,

here we are,
all her relatives who cared enough
to take a picture of her in this condition,
partying hard.

As far as I'm concerned,
I'm flying high.
I'll never be alone.
I might not die.
I tweet and Facebook hard.
I Instagram.
I aim. I pose. I post,
therefore I am.

The thing about death
is that it's undefeated.
Know this:
You will lose.

ALBUM

You will also be the dead relative
of some young stranger who will ask:
Who was that, Grandpa?
And he will turn the page.

Do you want to make something invisible?
See it every day.

SANTURCE

I see him again in the rearview mirror:
barefoot on the burning asphalt,
dried up, emaciated,
with no skin on one forearm.
A lush mustache like Nietzche's
blankets his blond and scarce teeth.
He is a shadow in the rain that consumes him.
His faded tattoos have drowned in his darkness.
He glances downward.
The city confines him
more than the prison that stole his spring.
His wife is but a bruised memory.
His child, now grown, anonymous,
also roams the streets by *Bellas Artes*
coughing up red.

The time for excellence
is now.

CERTAINTIES

No one awaits you in London.
You will waste another sabbatical.
Inertia quietly haunts you.
Someone will discard photographs of your past.
You will blindly reject the beauty
of a subtle woman.
Your books are laughable to the young.
The poetry you write today consumes you.
You suffer it purposelessly, sometimes on purpose.
The unfair memory of the face of your first love
has already vanished.
Time does not care about your exercise routine.
Orphanhood awaits you.
You will lose, irreparably,
landscapes, hope, loyal dogs.
You will not return to you.
You will uselessly chase
what you once considered irrelevant.
And you will not be the protagonist
of your own funeral.

You seem
so perfect
now
that you are gone.

WAKE

I envy your death.
The effectiveness of the drink, the news,
your pleased demeanor at the wake,
the simple obituary, the words
of those you left behind:
how much emptier he leaves this world,
it was so brief, etcetera. No one
could have predicted your absence.
It was the ideal moment
to pause,
to strap the veil of night on your biography.

And here I am so envious of your death
and its untimeliness, your death
and its impetuousness
because you stole my role,
the dead man's position,
the drama of the tears,
the stunned stares, the pain.

You stole my death
and for that I detest you,

but grief breeds new perspectives,
and in the right angle of my body and yours,
your end becomes my practice,
your coffin is my model.
I never loved you more than as a corpse.

"Why are you depressed?"

"Why are you not?"

WEAK SPOT

Precisely after choosing
the method and the hour,
and sharpening the blade
and finishing the letter
—a brief epitaph crafted in thirteen days—
he shaved his legs, his arms, his armpits,
his abdomen, his chest, his cranium;
he shaved his back, his pubis, his testicles.
With the edge of the blade on his temple
bit by bit
he shaved each eyebrow.

As he saw his reflection in the mirror,
he thought it was a stranger,
and thus it would not be
suicide. It would be murder.
Enthralled by his new hairlessness,
he took his time to enter his mother's bathtub.
Finally he submerged his trembling legs
into the hot water.
He managed to sit down in the full tub,

and just before he used the blade
to penetrate his liver or some vein,
he felt a pair of gums biting his heel:
a tiny frog was there
keeping him company.

Call your mother.
Now.

BRIGHT DAY

It is summer.
On the street, children play hide-and-go-seek.
The ice cream man arrives pushing his cart.
Bronzed joggers sprint with cadence.
The neighbor weeds her garden.
The smell of fresh-cut grass and vanilla
emanates from your carport. The Jehova's
Witnesses carry on seeking new prey.
The youngster in the corner waves to them
before his work commute.
Pigeons mock the stray cats.
An old man and his old dog
walk slowly on the opposite side
of a child who rides a bike.
Your next-door neighbor mixes soap and water
to wash his car. The trees
simulate his arms' hurricane sway.
Leaves fall like fainting frogs.
The sun keeps shining.
A stream of frigid water hits your skin.
The bathtub floods.
And no one has found out that you are dead.

All my life, my father
was afraid of dogs.
Why he became a mailman
is a mystery.

Notes on the Death of My Father

I

I heard it and just sighed.
Armed with a fictitious, inexplicable calm,
I went to his bedroom and opened his closet.
The scent of his skin betrayed me.
I chose the navy blue necktie,
his only suit, black,
and the white shirt. I ironed it
and starched
his absence with my tears.

II

Of the vast selection of boxes,
I decided that brown with copper lines
was the best, although it was the second cheapest one,
according to the salesman with the saddest of faces
and the heaviest of mustaches.
The tiny mortician asked

how my father combed his hair.
Back, I said to him.
                        Good, he replied.
And I gave the clothes to him.

III

There in the coffin,
inert, consumed, and clear,
he rested in defeat. I asked for his blessing.
I remember having touched
the almost imperceptible scar on his knuckle
from the scratch of the cat that still awaits him.
I held his hand and looked at him again,
and his face was my face.

IV

I regret that we never bid farewell,
that he didn't see me wed,
that my mother is alone with the cat.
I wish I'd had more patience
when, fragile, he was losing

the battle with his body.
I would walk with him at his slow pace
and feed him his oatmeal in the old spoon
that he always preferred.
And of so many words that I could say to him,
if I could,
I would say that now I understand
why he left.

"Daddy, I like to sleep on your warm arm.
Love,
Oscar."

THREE

I am my father,
and my father,
who dwells in the amnesia
that is grief,
returns to become me.
It all returns.
Yesterday awaits us in the future.

I am my son,
and my son
inexplicably,
thoroughly,
without having predicted it,
without remedy,
is my father, too.

"You're so exotic!
I like the way you talk with your hands.
And I love your tan."

THE TROUBLE WITH MY NAME

All my life I had been mispronouncing my name,
which I thought was Javier Ávila,
until I moved to Pennsylvania to learn linguistics
outside the classroom.

First came the tennis club experience:
"Hi, may I help you?" the nice lady asked.
"Yes, I have a court reserved for 2:00 pm," I replied.
"Under what name?"
"Ávila."
"Do you mean Aveela?"
(pause)
"Yes. That's what I meant."
And I thought, how nice of her to teach me
the proper pronunciation of my name.
It baffled me, though, because my publisher has
called me "Ávəla" for seven years.

My student, who wrote "Availa" on his first paper,
seemed surprised
when I suggested that he look at the syllabus

to read the proper spelling of my name,
and when he handed in his second paper
and said, "I got the name right this time,"
and I saw that he had written "Availa" again,
I told him that we never stop learning,
and he grinned as though he had never
heard sarcasm before.

The police officer who pulled me over
for having tinted windows,
said, "I'm gonna let this slide
because they're not so dark, Mr. Avilar."
And when I corrected him, he said,
"That might be the way Spanish people say it,
but this is America."
And who am I to tell him
that I am not Spanish,
or that America consists of dozens of countries,
and in most of them *se habla español?*

The principal at my son's school
prides herself in saying the students' names
correctly.
Therefore, when she said, "Mr. Aveea,
we'd be honored if you could come
and read poetry to the children,"
I naturally accepted,

in part because she didn't call me Mr. Avilia,
like the parent who recommended me did.

You see, I like that they have options,
that they can be creative,
that they will bravely forego
looking it up or asking the person
who has had the name for forty years or so.

But the real trouble, as it turns out,
is my first name.

Waiting for my license,
the DMV lady yelled, "Jayvier!"
And I had to look around to realize
that she meant me.

When I was hired to teach a writing workshop,
my future colleague
shook my hand and said,
"Welcome to the department, Javié!"
And it made me feel so nice and French.

At a conference, a fellow writer introduced me
to his friends as the Puerto Rican poet laureate,
JAvier, and to hear the first syllable
stressed so dactylically,

transported me to a Longfellow masterpiece.

The first time my chiropractor called me "Javeer,"
I went through an ethnic crisis,
but that was resolved when ten minutes later
the massage therapist said,
"Let's see how much stress
you've been holding onto, Javiray."

And of course, I felt something was fishy
when the mc at a poetry festival
introduced me as Dr. Javiar.

Getting takeout is an issue.
When they ask, "What's the name?"
I panic. What should be
my takeout alter ego?

Even Siri gets confused with me,
and we have an intimate relationship.
I mean, why go to the gym every day
if she insists on calling me Heavier?

You see, when my friends moved to the States,
they became other people instantly,
without alternate pronunciations:
Iván Vélez became Ivan Velez.

Joel Ramos became Joel Ramos.
And Brenda Aguirre became Brenda Aguirre.

I, on the other hand,
became many people every day,
and I still do.
There seems to be no cure
for my multiple name pronunciation disorder,
but there is a prescription that can heal it,
one that must be renewed daily
by phone.
So every day, I dial the number,
the only one I'll always know by heart,
and as soon as she answers the phone,
I hear my name the way it is supposed to sound:
in the voice of my mother.

I treat myself to a can of Old Colony pineapple soda
when I am in the Old Colony.

PUERTO RICAN MILITARY CONTRACT
FOR THE UNITED STATES ARMY

To Be Signed Immediately.

I can die for your country
but I can't vote
for your president.

"I don't see color, Javier.
I just see you as a good person.
Who cares where you're from?
Don't you think we should all get
beyond this race thing already?"

BACK IN THE GOOD OLD DAYS

Back in the good old days,
women couldn't vote
and had no access to a college education
or a career.

Back in the good old days,
a negro could be stoned to death
for moving into a white neighborhood,
and segregated water fountains
saved humans from colored disease.

Back in the good old days,
the white man who raped my black
great grandmother
never spent a minute in prison
and lived to do it again and again
to her and others.

Back in the good old days
our people were lynched
for the color of our skin,

and our owners believed
we should be grateful for being brought
from Africa to America.

Back in the good old days,
we had no voice.
This is how we learned
what it meant
to have privilege.

Privilege
is being able to say:
"I want my country back."

More Puerto Ricans
live in the U.S. mainland
than on the island.
Where on earth
is home?

DEBT

To part,
to leave behind the life
we know, to join the sea
of loss, to earn oblivion,
to taste uncertainty,
to pierce it,
to recognize the urgency
of now

is what we owe
the future.

Grammar matters. Punctuation matters.
Imagine if you were to omit the comma from the song,
"Come on, Eileen."
Eileen might not like it.

GRADER FEAR

PORTRAIT OF AN ENGLISH PROFESSOR
GRADING PAPERS
ON A SUNDAY EVENING

5:45

The missing apostrophe
would be a minor offense
if it were not in the first word
of the title.

6:30

The tribute poem for Lynn's grandmother
has taken a turn for the worse:
"I remember her genital touch
as she lay in bed, dying."
You can almost forgive the misspelling
that makes the piece horrifying
because Lynn has understood

the concept of enjambment,
and she has conjugated "lie"
properly
at last.

8:15

You wonder what grade Bryan
earned in English I,
now that he is in your English II class
dropping knowledge on immigration:
"Its America your suppose to speak english
if you dont like it than go back to Mexico, were you
belong
you can speak spanish their and nobody we'll judge
you
we want are country back."
English is Bryan's first and only language.
He owns five guns. This fall he gave you venison.
A gift. The note, "Your awesome," moved you,
despite the second part: "eventhou your mexican."
And when you told him your nationality,
he laughed in disbelief, "There ain't no Ricans
teaching English in the States."

10:23

After a dozen essays, you return
to verse, to Leslie's heartbreak.
The poetic accident,
"I never meant to heart you,"
precedes her equally stunning,
"I love you with all my hurt,"
in a piece that makes up
what it lacks in imagery
with a genuine dispelling
of love.

12:03

"Three more," you tell yourself
as you turn another page.
Literature and the Environment
seemed like a good idea at the time,
but who could have predicted
the fervor
of the climate change denier?
In All Caps, he explodes:

"COME ON OBAMA!
WAKE UP PEOPLE!
OPEN YOUR EYES!"
If this passionate plea
were to be followed,
what should happen first?

12:54

After much abuse
of mind and sight,
it happens, and you must
reread that final statement:
"Us American's have a bright future a head."
Suddenly, tears
—glorious, patriotic tears—
descend.

1:30
In your nightmare, a man with impeccable grammar
slits your throat.
You smile.

First, listen.
The past is whispering in your ear.

BLOODLINE

for Oscar

Abuela Vene,
the daughter of a former slave and her owner,
married a Spaniard who became
a Puerto Rican Nationalist,
and together, amid the dangers
of Albizu's battles,
they had three sons—
the youngest of which, Alfonso,
treasured me the way I treasure you.
You carry the heart of West Africa,
the might of Spain,
the dream of independence
in your veins.

Abuela Juana,
whose parents can be traced back
to the natives who greeted Columbus,
married Gracia, a blue-eyed campesino,
and of their eleven children,

my mother, Josefina,
the first to attend college,
would sweat through a two-hour commute
on three buses, in the sweltering heat of the tropics
to become a teacher.
The nobility of the Taíno
and the grit of the jíbaro
shine in you.

Great grandma Bernadine,
daughter of Austro-Hungarian immigrants
who severed their Slavic roots
amid the turmoil of war,
lost her husband as a young mother,
and raised her three children by herself.
Her oldest, Nancy,
who cultivated kindness
from the hardship of scarcity,
gave birth to your mother.
The resilience of the Slovak
who survived against the odds,
against the elements,
propels you.

Great grandma Genevieve,
Irish, life of the party,
and your Polish American great grandfather,

a mailman, like my father,
taught Grandpa Joe, the oldest of seven,
the meaning of honest work,
and within you,
the unyielding spirit of Ireland
and the fortitude of Poland
coexist.

A convergence of countries
has shaped your history.
Some roads that led you here
were paved with blood,
most often shed in vain.
Up north, brave women and brave men
fled the only worlds they knew
in search of something better for their children.
Toward the island, it was a different journey
for the *conquistadores*
who ravaged, built, and altered a land
that they would lose after 400 years
to a country that still cannot understand
the splendor of our race,
the anarchy of hearts that ache for sovereignty,
a state that can't be found.

Our people are all from somewhere else,
but they are all from here.

From the treacherous distances they traveled,
with the courage to build another legacy,
unquestionably something has emerged,
and that, my son, is hope.

You are every slave that worked the fields
and dreamt of being free.
Every Irishman and Pole who was spat on
by immigrants that came before them
and by each other,
weathering unmerciful winters,
breaking their backs working the mines and farms.
You are every newcomer
who changed his name to assimilate;
who disposed of his native language to assimilate;
who was told that being an American
is to assimilate;
who, by stripping his heritage
and grieving it in silence,
waited for the warmth of equal treatment.

You are every Puerto Rican
who left the sugar cane field
for a mainland factory job making lowly wages
and awaiting equal treatment
from fellow American citizens
who refuse to see.

You, *hijo*, are every tear
of the Taíno whose land
was ripped away by greed,
disease, and hate.
You are all of them, their truth,
and the distortions of their truth,
the centuries, the continents,
the oceans, seas, and rivers
that flow into your being, and reflect
the rainbow that has spread into your eyes,
where in chaotic harmony
they celebrate at last,
and in a multitude of languages
they scream:

"I am the future of America!
I am the future of America!
I am the future of America!
When you see me,
You'll see yourself."

The author would like to thank
the following people for making
the one-man show possible:

Karen Paddock
Josefina Morales
Michelle Cintrón
Adam Atkinson
Samuel Medina
Nancy Paddock
Joseph Paddock
Jean Marie Stack
Oscar Ávila

Javier Ávila (San Juan, Puerto Rico) is the recipient of the Instituto de Cultura Puertorriqueña Poetry Award (*The Dead Man's Position*, 2010), the Pen Club Book of the Year Award (*The Symmetry of Time, 2005*), and the Olga Nolla Poetry Award—twice, for *Broken Glass under the Carpet* (2003) and *The Symmetry of Time* (2005). His best-selling novel *Different* (2001) earned him critical acclaim and was made into a movie entitled *Miente* (2009). Two of his other novels, *The Professor in Ruins* (2006) and the controversial *La profesión más antigua (The Oldest Profession, 2012)*, explore Puerto Rico's academic underworld. *Criatura del olvido (Creature of Oblivion)* was awarded another PEN Club Poetry Award in 2008. That same year, Ávila was honored with the prestigious Outstanding Latino Cultural Arts, Literary Arts and Publications Award given by the American Association of Hispanics in Higher Education. Ávila's dual-language anthology *Vapor* (2014) brings together poems from his four award-winning books. In his novel *Polvo (Dust,* 2017), a devious man uncovers chilling secrets that transform his life. Ávila, who teaches literature and writing at Northampton Community College, received the 2015 Pennsylvania Professor of the Year Award by the Carnegie Foundation for the Advancement of Teaching and the Council for Advancement and Support of Education. He is the first Latino to receive this honor.